Jonah
God of the
second chance

Jonah

God of the
second chance

SELWYN
HUGHES

Contents

Introduction

One writer describes the book of Jonah as 'everybody's favourite'. Children love the story of Jonah, as do adults – both Christian and non-Christian. He is best known, of course, for the dramatic encounter he had with 'a great fish'. One preacher commented: 'Put Jonah in the middle of a bunch of anglers and you can be sure of one thing – his story of the one that got away will beat all the others!'

Many who have read or heard the story of Jonah regard it as a fictitious tale or a parable designed to correct unspiritual attitudes. They put it in the same category as such stories as Moby Dick, Pinocchio or the Arabian Nights – fascinating but fictional. However, if you read 2 Kings 14:23–29 you will see quite clearly that Jonah was a real person – a prophet who lived during the days of Jeroboam II (793–753 BC) and predicted the expansion of the northern kingdom of Israel: '… the word of the LORD … spoken through his servant Jonah son of Amittai, the prophet from Gath Hepher' (v.25). A grave near Nazareth is still pointed out to tourists as that of the prophet Jonah.

Though Jonah was right in some of the things he did, many aspects of his life were not praiseworthy. If Jonah is not a model to emulate, why are we studying his life and why is his story included in the Old Testament? Eugene Peterson claims the reason is to give us training in humility – 'a humility which turns out to be not grovelling but cheerful'. I think you will find that in this detailed study of the book of Jonah, though we are focusing on a man whose life in many ways seems a failure, the lessons we learn from his attitudes and actions will help us to fail less.

01

Saying 'no' to God
Jonah 1:1–3

*'But Jonah ran away from the
LORD ...'*

(Jonah 1:3)

o

o

o

The Jonah story begins with the fact that he is given a task to perform which he doesn't want: Having received a prophetic call to preach in Nineveh (1:2), he plans to head in the opposite direction. Jonah didn't object to preaching, but he wanted to choose his own pulpit! Nineveh was the great capital of the ancient Assyrian Empire and was built on the banks of the Tigris River in north-eastern Mesopotamia, which we know today as Iraq.

The Assyrians were enemies of Israel, and their brutality and wickedness was such that it offended the sensitive heart of God. 'Go to Nineveh,' says the Almighty to Jonah, 'and thunder in their ears that their wickedness is known to me' (v.2, Moffatt). Why should God worry about one of Israel's fiercest enemies? Jonah is nonplussed by God's sudden interest in them and fails to understand why He should attempt to save such evil people. But shouldn't a prophet obey God's commands without question or quibble? We would think so, but Jonah is adamant. This is one job he can do without.

Put yourself in Jonah's place. Would you be willing to follow the Lord's clear command if He asked you to do something that to you didn't seem to make sense? How many of us, I wonder – whether we are prophets or not – pull back from doing what God asks us because it appears to be against our better judgment? I have been in that situation many times in my life and so I imagine have you. Those who commit themselves to serving the Lord must come to grips with this most important fact: we are not called to understand but to stand. Those who can't or won't grasp this truth make little progress along the path of discipleship.

We are not called to understand but to stand.

What were the reasons for Jonah's noncompliance? Did he fear for his life? Was he overcome by cowardice?

Personally, I think that his disinclination to follow God's instructions (1:3) was due to being overly concerned for his own reputation. A later statement indicates this was certainly a factor (4:2).

The people of Israel had seen many prophets come and go. On more than one occasion in the nation's history men had claimed to be prophets even though they had no call from God. In the time of Moses God had warned that this would happen and had given instructions on how to differentiate between the false and the true: 'If what a prophet proclaims in the name of the LORD does not take place or come true, that is a message the LORD has not spoken' (Deut. 18:22). I have no doubt Jonah pondered the fact that if, after prophesying against Nineveh, the people repented, causing God to refrain from dispensing judgment, then some might conclude he was not a true prophet. His concern was not for God and His glory but for his own reputation.

Sin has been described as putting our ego in the place where God wants to be. Sigmund Freud said his whole teaching could best be summed up in the phrase: 'Where Id [the sum total of our instinctive impulses] is, let Ego be.' The Christian philosophy, I believe, is best summed up in this phrase: Where ego is, let God be.

What God delights in

We pause to look at a text that shows the contrast between Jonah's attitude and the compassionate and forgiving nature of God, 'But you, O Lord, are a compassionate and gracious God, slow to anger, abounding in love and faithfulness' (Psa. 86:15).

As the events of Jonah's story unfold, it becomes quite clear that he was more interested in pronouncing judgment than in announcing the offer of divine forgiveness. Many believers I have met are like that; they are fiery in their denunciation of sin but fail to emphasise the fact that the thing God delights to do is to forgive.

Some time ago I gave a lecture for the Bible Society in Dublin on the subject 'The Bible – God's Word for Today'. After I had completed my lecture, a Catholic priest commented on the statement I had made concerning the truth that God delights to forgive. He said, 'If an angel came down into this room tonight and told us that the Trinity had decided to abandon the fact of hell, many of us would be very disappointed, as we all know people we would like to see finish up there.' The audience laughed, but they identified with the point he was making.

How many of us, I wonder, gain a sense of moral satisfaction from the thought that sinful people deserve judgment when we should be concentrating on their need for forgiveness? Let us be quite clear about this: God is against sin – all sin – and promises that the unrepentant will be punished. But what He loves to do is forgive. Listen to what God says through the prophet Micah: 'What does the LORD require of you? To act justly and to love mercy ...' (Micah 6:8). Perhaps we ought to still our hearts for a moment and ask ourselves this crucial question: Am I as concerned about mercy as I am about judgment?

The Tarshish illusion

It is interesting to notice that in response to God's command Jonah sets off, but he sets off in the wrong direction. He could have ignored God's call and remained where he was, continuing with the familiar routines, but instead he sets out for Tarshish (1:3). Why Tarshish?

Well, for one thing, Tarshish was a much more exciting proposition than Nineveh. The Tarshish spoken of here was most likely the Spanish town called Tartessus which was famous for its silver, iron, tin and lead. The city exported these minerals to such places as Joppa and Tyre. Ezekiel speaks of the trade which the people of Tyre had with Spain: 'Tarshish did business with you because of your great wealth of goods' (Ezek. 27:12). Nineveh was an ancient city with an unhappy history; Tarshish promised adventure. My Bible dictionary says that in Old Testament times Tarshish, in the popular imagination, became a kind of distant paradise – Shangri la.

I wonder, am I talking to someone who has been called by God to do something which seems difficult? If so, do you find yourself contemplating moving in the opposite direction to that which you have been called? Are you just about to buy a ticket to 'Tarshish'? For all of you lined up at the travel agents I have this message: your attempt to escape from God's call is just not worth it. You can run but you can't hide. The Lord knows the end from the beginning, and though He loves you as you are, He loves you too much to let you stay as you are. Jonah ran, but God ran after him. Be careful when you find yourself in circumstances that seem to aid you in your flight from God's commands. Conducive conditions are not necessarily indicators of the divine will.

The travel ticket which Jonah purchased from Joppa to Tarshish was, without doubt, one of the costliest ever acquired. He moved in the opposite direction to that stipulated by God and finished up in the deep. Let's remind ourselves of the circumstances. God commands Jonah to go to Nineveh, a city over 500 miles north-east of Jerusalem. Instead, Jonah sets out for a port probably in Spain – a city that lay in an opposite direction.

There is just no point in going against God's will – that is not where success lies. A motto on the wall of the Bible college where I trained read: 'To be in the will of God is better than success.' Some students met one evening and had a discussion. 'There is something not quite right about that statement,' they commented. 'It would be better to say: "To be in the will of God *is* success".' Everyone agreed and, after approaching the principal, the motto was changed. Had Jonah reached Tarshish he might have had a seemingly successful life, but it would have been 'success' that lay outside the will of God, therefore unsuccess. *Success, for a believer, is knowing the will of God – and doing it.*

Jonah paid heavily for running away from God. And so will we. On the outside we may appear to be carefree, but on the inside we will pay the price in inner conflicts such as guilt, anxiety and so on. Someone has said we are not so much punished for our sins as by our sins. When we try to disregard something God has called us to do we cannot really escape – either from God or ourselves. All that results is that we cannot live with God. And if we cannot live with God then we won't be able to live with ourselves.

God is everywhere

Jonah 1:3 begins and ends with the statement that Jonah was running away from the Lord. It starts, 'But Jonah ran away from the LORD', and it finishes, 'and sailed to Tarshish to flee from the LORD'. The two statements beg the question: Why would anyone want to run away from the Lord? Or: Can anyone really run away from the Lord?

It seems Jonah had an imperfect view of God and His presence. The prevailing opinion in many nations during Old Testament times was that each country's god was limited to its own land. Sometimes people would carry soil from one country to another in the belief that the god of that country would travel with them. The story of Naaman's quest for healing demonstrates this kind of thinking (2 Kings 5:17). Some Israelites believed that God was confined to the Temple in Jerusalem or, at most, to the territory of Israel. So perhaps

Jonah thought that when he sailed away from the shores of Israel he would be leaving God behind. Or he may have thought that when he got far away from Israel, then the impact of God's presence would be diminished in his life, in the same way that a radio signal fades the further one gets from the transmitter. Jonah would learn, as we must learn, that there is nowhere where God is not.

There is nowhere where God is not.

I once read the story of a militant atheist who wrote on a wall the words: 'God is nowhere.' But unwittingly he left a space between the letters 'w' and 'h'. As he stood back and looked at what he had written he read: 'God is now here.' It brought about his conversion.

Further Study

Rom. 15:4; 1 Cor. 10:13; 2 Tim. 3:16; 2 Pet. 1:20–21

1. Why were people's failures included in the Old Testament?
2. What can we learn from them?

1 Cor. 3:18–4:13; Gal. 2:19–20; Phil. 2:1–8

3. Why are people so concerned with reputation?
4. What was Christ's example?

Deut. 10:12–13; 11:1–32; Josh. 1:6–9; Psa. 84:10

5. Why does God give us commands?
6. Does transgression bring punishments or consequences?

02

Saved by a storm
Jonah 1:4–6

'Then the LORD sent a great
wind on the sea.'
(Jonah 1:4)

o

o

o

Jonah, on his voyage to Tarshish, finds himself in stormy weather: 'Then the LORD sent a great wind on the sea ...' (v.4). The hurricane ruined his plans to go to Tarshish; his vacation was spoiled but his vocation was saved. None of us likes to find ourself caught up in a storm, but sometimes this is the only way God can get our attention. George Herbert, in his book *The Country Parson*, has these lines:

> *Poets have wrong'd poor storms; such days are best,*
> *They purge the air without, within the breast.*

A storm may bring chaos and cause great damage but it also clears the air.

I once talked to a man who told me that he had gone through a period of deep psychological depression. He described this time as like being in a storm. My curiosity was aroused when he concluded, 'Now I can thank God for my depression.' I asked him **'Storms are the triumph of His art.'** how he could thank God for depression, and his reply went something like this, 'My depression was due to wrong patterns of living. I needed those wrong patterns and ideas shaken up and challenged, for they were sending my life in the wrong direction. The depression was a message that said, "You are not thinking right, or living right. I am going to turn your life upside down and inside out. You won't like it for a while, but it will be for your ultimate good." I came out of the storm a new man.'

Though it may be difficult for us to admit it, the truth is that some of us cling to things that will be loosened only by a storm. Another of the lines from *The Country Parson* which I love is this: 'Storms are the triumph of His art.' They are.

All knees on deck

The sailors on board the ship bound for Tarshish had to encounter two storms: one was on the sea, the other was in their hearts. These sailors had had plenty of experience at sea and no doubt had been buffeted by many storms, but this one was different. As they listened to the wind and the sound of the creaking timbers, and saw the huge waves breaking over them, they were terrified. But what could they do in such a desperate situation? Well, they could pray. I am not sure if the captain ordered 'all knees on deck', but each one, we are told, cried out to his own god (1:5).

The sailors were not only a praying party but a practical group also. Perhaps they believed in the old adage that God helps those who help themselves. Across the howling hurricane they shout to each other, 'Let's lighten the load.' And, in order to lessen the danger, they throw the cargo overboard (1:5). After all, what is the value of corn when compared to human lives?

We must remember, of course, that these men were praying to non-existent gods, but the point that prayer must go hand in hand with action is still valid. There is a passive side to prayer and an active side also. The taking from God must lead to undertaking for God. The quiet must quicken. These lines make the point most effectively:

> *You must use your hands while praying, though,*
> *If an answer you would get,*
> *For prayer-worn knees and a rusty hoe*
> *Never raised a big crop yet.*

A definition of prayer I have always liked is this: prayer is receptivity. But if prayer were only receptivity then we would be left leaning too much towards the passive side of life. We would be left (as I've pointed out) with the attitude of taking without undertaking. I would remind you again that although the sailors were praying to non-existent gods, they put 'hands and feet' to their prayers. They were prayerful but creative.

Every believer should find prayer to be creative, for when our lesser life touches the Life it becomes alive – alive to the fingertips. Frequently I reflect on the passage in the New Testament that tells of Jesus getting up early, while it was still dark, and going off to a solitary place to pray. Simon Peter searches for Him and when he finds Him, says, 'Everyone is looking for you.' Jesus replies, 'Let us go ... so that I can preach' (Mark 1:35–38). Our Lord's praying was preaching in incubation. The praying stimulated the preaching, the receptivity became response, the impression of the prayer hour became the expression of the preaching hour.

The most effective Christians in the world are those who wait quietly before God in prayer and then rise to put their hands to the practical tasks that await them. The poised, prayerful person becomes sure of directions, sure of their resources and moves from task to task with calm confidence. The prayerless are hurried, flurried and worried. They wear themselves out with their frictions.

Oranges versus diamonds

Reflecting still on the fact that the sailors on the ship headed for Tarshish thought nothing of tipping the whole cargo into the sea, it has been said that 'Trouble helps us more than anything to see things in their true perspective.' Possessions don't count for much when one's life is at stake.

Many years ago, on the night of 14 April 1912 to be precise, the *Titanic*, the largest vessel then afloat, crashed into an iceberg in mid-Atlantic, and four hours later sank to the bottom of the ocean. A good deal has been written of all that took place in those four hours. Survivors spoke of the calm heroism of the captain, the officers and the crew. They told of the courage of the bandmaster, who led the playing of 'Nearer my God to Thee'. They told another story also, less courageous but equally interesting. A certain wealthy woman, who had been allotted a place in one of the lifeboats, asked if she might run back to her cabin to get something, and was given three minutes to go. She hurried along the corridors which were already tilting at a dangerous angle. When she reached her cabin she saw money and costly gems littering the floor. She saw them, but she paid no attention. Snatching at two oranges, she ran back to the lifeboat. Hours before, who would have said the moment would come when she might prefer two oranges to valuable jewels? But death had boarded the *Titanic*, and with one blast of its awful breath reversed her values. Oranges were worth more than diamonds.

Trouble, storm trouble, forces us to identify the essentials – it helps us see things as they really are. 'Set your minds on things above, not on earthly things' (Col 3:2).

Jonah the escapist

How strange, that while the sailors were frantically trying to keep the vessel afloat, Jonah was below deck – fast asleep (1:5). Jesus, you will remember, was also in a boat when a storm blew up (Mark 4:35–41). And He, too, fell asleep – but for a different reason. His sleep was due to physical tiredness. Jonah's was due to a psychological condition known as escapism. He escaped into sleep.

Escapism has been described as 'the attempt to avoid difficult situations or uncomfortable feelings ... by withdrawing or engaging in thoughts or behaviours which tend to draw the mind away from the thing feared'. Some escape into illness. I must emphasise that not all forms of illness are an attempt to escape from reality, but a number are. This idea might at first be difficult to accept, as certain illnesses can be deeply distressing. People I have talked to whose illness was clearly the result of escapism have said to me, 'Why would I retreat into illness when my condition is so physically troublesome?' The answer is that the mind diverts attention from mental or emotional pain by producing a physical one. Sometimes a physical pain can be easier to handle. Psychologists have a term for this: conversion. The mind converts a mental or emotional problem to a physical one.

A man I once counselled complained that he couldn't wake up in the mornings. After nine or more hours' sleep he had to be woken by his wife. Yet his doctor had told him there was no physical reason for his condition. After talking to him, I found he was carrying a lot of unresolved conflicts. One by one they were dealt with, and within days he returned to a normal sleep pattern. When he had nothing to retreat from he woke up fresh and eager to face the day.

A prayerless prophet

In a storm it is a matter of 'all hands on deck', but two hands, at least, in this instance, were missing – Jonah's. The prophet's hands were folded, not in prayer, but to form a cushion on which to sleep. He was discovered by the captain, who woke him. ' "What do you mean," he roared, "sleeping at a time like this? Get up and cry to your god, and see if he will have mercy on us and save us!" ' (1:6, TLB).

Though the captain's rebuke must have brought Jonah to his feet, there is no record of him calling on God in prayer. How could he explain to the captain that he was not on speaking terms with his God? How different from Jesus who, when He was woken by His disciples in the midst of a fierce squall, rose to His feet, prayed to His Father and commanded the storm to cease (Mark 4:39). We said that storms reveal what we value in life, and in this storm Jonah is exposed as a man who didn't regard prayer as important. An elderly Welsh preacher of my acquaintance used to define prayer as 'revision'. Why revision? Because, as he put it, 'a revised version of your life is put out every time you pray – really pray'. When we open up our heart to God then more and more of our life is brought under His control and is pruned.

Storms reveal what we value in life.

A Christian psychologist once undertook some research into the matter of what causes Christians to lapse into prayerlessness. He found that the chief reason was that they were harbouring things in their hearts they did not want to give up. They knew that if they prayed, God would have an opportunity to challenge them about these matters. When you want to hold on to guilt, self-pity, resentment and such like, then it is better not to pray.

As we said, when we open up our heart to God in prayer then we are bringing more of our life under His control and consequently, as channels of receptivity are opened, our will is brought into alignment with the will of God.

Education has been defined as change. If this is so, then prayer is life's greatest form of education, for through prayer we are being educated at the place that counts – at the centre of life. We are being educated in being.

Dear Lord, three things I pray:
To see Thee more clearly,
Love Thee more dearly,
Follow Thee more nearly,
Day by day.

If prayer is revision, then prayer involves pruning. 'He ... cleans every branch which does bear fruit, to make it bear richer fruit' (John 15:2, Moffatt). Cleans it of what? He cleans it of suckers that sap the life of the branch, suckers that bear no fruit, that only keep the branch from bearing fruit. It is because of this that when Christians say to me they are too busy to pray I respond, 'Then you are busier than God intends you to be.'

Further Study

Job 1:1–17; 2:7–3:26; 32:1–2; 42:1–17

1. How did Job's storm clear the air?
2. How was the storm for his ultimate good?

Ezra 7:10; Neh. 4:9; Esth. 4:16; Matt. 9:36–10:8

3. How is prayer and action linked?
4. What were the disciples to do?

1 Sam. 10:19–24; 1 Kings 19:1–19; Psa. 55:3–8

5. What is escapism?
6. Is there anything you are trying to escape?

03

Lying to yourself
Jonah 1:7–12

*'Come, let us cast lots to find
out who is responsible for
this calamity.'*

(Jonah 1:7)

o
o
o

When Jonah is persuaded to come on deck he sees the sailors engaged in feverish discussion with each other. For all their prayers to their different gods, the storm is as bad as ever. So many people are praying, but the storm does not diminish. What is the reason for this, they ask themselves. Eventually they conclude that the storm is some form of punishment, that someone has angered the gods. But who is the person responsible? They cast lots to find out (1:7). In those superstitious days it was customary, when the use of reason and logic failed to settle an issue, to mark a pebble and put it in a bag along with several unmarked pebbles. The individual who drew out the marked pebble was viewed as being responsible for the matter in question.

While the drawing of lots is being organised, Jonah holds his peace. He knows something which nobody else knows, but he stays silent. Why doesn't he own up and say, 'There is no need to cast lots. I'm the culprit ... I'm the one responsible for this storm'? Was it cowardice? I don't think so. Clearly, Jonah's conscience wasn't working in the way it should at this point. It had been dulled by self-pity and by his prayerless condition.

I can think of nothing more injurious to the spiritual life than having a conscience that does not operate in the way it was designed. King David deceived himself to such an extent that his conscience failed to function correctly until God brought Nathan to him with a barbed parable that penetrated his defences and helped him see himself as he really was (2 Sam. 12:1–14). Any man or woman whose conscience does not move with speed and certainty is like a ship at sea without a compass.

If we look a little deeper into why Jonah kept quiet I think there was another reason: he was lying to himself.

Now lying of any kind is to be strongly condemned and must inevitably result in spiritual loss (see Jer. 9:5). But if I were forced to decide which kind of lying is worst, I would unhesitatingly declare that it is lying to oneself. This leads by scarcely perceptible degrees to the worst state into which a man or woman may fall. I once heard Dr Sangster, one of Methodism's greatest preachers, say this:

> At first it might sound absurd to speak of lying to oneself. Men and women lie to deceive somebody who is unacquainted with the facts. It is usually a cowardly device for concealing the unpleasant truth from a person at present in ignorance, and hence it seems possible only to lie to somebody who has less information upon the point than you have yourself. If they knew the truth as you knew it, you couldn't deceive them. How, then, can a man or woman lie to themselves?

Such arguments will be used only by those who are ignorant of the cunning of the human heart.

The truth is that we can and do lie to ourselves, and I suspect we all know something of the danger from personal experience. Jonah stood on the deck with a dulled conscience and believing a self-imposed lie. And what was that lie? Perhaps this: 'I am not the only one to blame ... others are bad too.'

We can and do lie to ourselves.

How should we deal with people whose consciences are dulled and who have deceived themselves to such an extent that they will not own up to their lapsed spiritual condition? It is a big problem. If you argue with them, they argue back. And usually they are not lacking in specious arguments. Even before you begin they are on the defensive and they fight every step of the way. If you fall back on flat affirmation and exclaim, 'Surely you can see what is happening to you,' they will say something along these lines: 'There is more than one way of looking at things,' or, 'I'm only human ... everybody fails from time to time.' And if you still persist, they turn away from you with an air of injured dignity.

In the case of King David, as we have mentioned, God brought to him the prophet Nathan whose carefully crafted story got beneath his defences and exposed his self-deception (2 Sam. 12:1–14). Runaways from God and His truth have to be outmanoeuvred. If Jonah would not own up to his spiritual condition and admit that the storm was God's way of bringing him to his senses, then God would find some other way to deal with him. God watched as the sailors cast lots and intervened at the right moment to make sure that 'the lot fell on Jonah' (1:7). The action was human but the outcome was divine.

Jonah must have thought that his chances of getting away with his crime were high, but what a shock he had when the lot showed him to be the culprit. An interesting verse in the book of Proverbs says, 'We toss the coin, but it is the LORD who controls its decision' (Prov. 16:33, TLB). When will we learn that there is just no way we can outmanoeuvre God?

Let me tell you a story

We pause to look at a psalm that Jonah would have done well to consider, Psalm 139. If he had prayed 'Search me, O God ... test me ... see if there is any offensive way in me' (Psa. 139:23) then he would have saved himself a great deal of difficulty. There are many degrees between a life lived with God and the complete moral collapse of a man like Jonah, but this extreme case has the merit of showing the vivid contrast. Have your feet strayed into the same perilous path as Jonah's? Are you lying to yourself? Let me warn you against doing so. Permit me to do as Nathan did with David and tell you a story.

There was once a man who was brought up in a good home, received training in the way of righteousness and had the reputation of being a fine Christian. But gradually things began to change and he found himself becoming more concerned about his work than what pleased God; spiritual matters began to take second place. He kept up the duties of the Christian life, said a prayer at the end of the day, faithfully read his Bible, but never admitted that what was being said applied to him. *Are you that man?*

There was once a young woman who was a bright and shining light for Jesus. Then she got married and had children. Gradually she began to lose her interest in spiritual matters, the fire in her life burned low, and she settled for spiritual mediocrity. She, too, read the Bible, but neatly deflected the truth onto other people. She thought of others who needed spiritual renewal; never herself. *Are you that woman?* If so, then I commend you to God who forgives, cleanses, restores and redeems.

Questions galore

As soon as Jonah is known to be the cause of the storm he is plagued by one question after another from the sailors (1:8–10). They fire them at him fast and furiously: 'What have you done to bring this awful storm upon us? Who are you? What is your work? What country are you from? What is your nationality?' (1:8, TLB). Jonah tells them that he is a Hebrew and a worshipper of the true God who made the sea and the land, and that he is running away from Him. This made them more terrified than ever, for they realised that they were harbouring a fugitive from the One who could, within minutes, turn a calm sea into a terrifyingly turbulent one. Why Jonah was running from his God they did not know, but they saw clearly from the howling hurricane and the raging sea that He was a God to be reckoned with.

When we look at God's ways from the vantage point of the whole of Scripture we see that what drives Him is not the desire to battle with the human will and win, but benevolence and love. C.S. Lewis wrote in *The Problem of Pain* that 'when we want to be something other than the thing God wants for us to be, we must be wanting what in fact will not make us happy'. God knew that Jonah would never be fulfilled outside His will and He set about doing for him what he needed, not what he wanted. Some might consider it petulant of God to have chased Jonah when he wanted to get away, but a great tragedy would have occurred if God had allowed him to keep running. When you know God wants you to do something, don't run. God may not stop you as He did Jonah.

A God to be reckoned with.

God's loving disciplines

The fact is that God loves us too much not to discipline us. Personally, I have doubts about using the word 'punishment' in connection with a believer; a better word, I think, is 'discipline'. '... God disciplines us for our good, that we may share in his holiness' (Heb. 12:10). God was not so much punishing Jonah for the mentality that led him to run away but disciplining him so that he could still be used in the future.

Some might have difficulty with that statement and will see the whole story of Jonah as an expression of God's anger and petulance. But that is not so. Steven Covey, in his book *The Seven Habits of Effective People*, talks about the difference between a win-lose approach to life and a win-win attitude. The win-lose approach is evident when one person tries to get the better of another; the win-win approach is apparent when one person wants to win but is equally interested in the other person winning. God's approach to Jonah was that of win-win. He was not spelling out the message to Jonah, 'See how much bigger than you I am.' No, He wanted him back in the prophetic ministry and carrying His message to Nineveh.

Quoting again from *The Problem of Pain*: C.S. Lewis says, 'God has paid us the most intolerable compliment of loving us in the deepest, most tragic, most inexorable sense.' Sometimes God's disciplines seem harsh and unkind, but behind them is a heart that beats with love. He loves us too much to let us get away with things. The next time you feel that God is bullying you into submission then remember this: If He didn't love you so much He would not persist in the way He does. It may seem unacceptable to you but really it is a divine compliment.

Another form of escapism?

As the fury of the storm increases, the sailors want desperately to remedy the situation. If the storm is the result of a dispute between Jonah and his God then surely, they think, he will know what should be done. So the sailors ask him, 'What should we do to you to make the sea calm down for us?' (1:11). Jonah knows the answer. If the crew want to rid themselves of the trouble, they have to rid themselves of Jonah. 'Pick me up and throw me into the sea,' is his reply.

'I know that it is my fault that this great storm has come upon you' (1:12). Isn't it interesting that though Jonah was not willing to go to Nineveh, he was willing to be thrown overboard. What was in his mind, I wonder, when he made this statement? Regret at putting the sailors' lives at risk? A desire to have his life ended? An attempt to offer himself as a substitutionary sacrifice? Can Jonah's decision to be a scapegoat be compared to Moses' plea: 'Blot me out of the book you have written' (Exod. 32:32)? I don't think so. My own opinion is that Jonah was not yet repentant and was feeling sorry for himself rather than sorry for having disobeyed the Lord. One commentator suggests that Jonah's request to be thrown overboard was actually an act of penance. That may be so, but it was not penance that was needed at that moment; it was repentance. Was this another form of escapism? An attempt to dodge the real issue by substituting another?

An act of penance may be appropriate after one has received forgiveness, but it must never be thought of as *earning* forgiveness. There was only one way for Jonah to be restored, and that was not by being cast into the sea but by casting himself into the arms of a loving and merciful God. If only ...

We must make clear here what repentance really is. The word 'repent' in Greek is *metanoia*, which means 'a change of mind', or 'an about turn'.

C.S. Lewis described repentance as 'a movement of the soul that is full speed astern'. It is not fun to repent; when one repents the soul is at its most serious stance. And it is much more than eating humble pie, says Lewis. 'It means unlearning all the self-conceit and self-will that we have been training ourselves into for ... years. It means killing a part of yourself, undergoing a kind of death.' He points out also that this 'kind of death' is not something God demands of us before He will take us back; it is simply a description of what going back to Him is like. If we ask God to take us back without it, he says, then we are really asking Him to take us back without going back.

When I was last in India I saw a man who had bound himself in chains sitting outside the tent where I was due to speak. I asked the pastor who was escorting me why he was sitting there like that. 'He is attempting to pay a penance for his sins,' he explained. If he had come into the tent he would have heard that penance is not enough. Penance without repentance is mere self-punishment. That is what Jonah wanted to do – he wanted to provide his own atonement. Penance has a place in the Christian life but it always comes after repentance – never before it. The reversal of this important issue is 'another gospel'.

Further Study

Deut. 8:1–20; Psa. 94:12; Prov. 3:11–12; 15:5

1. What part does discipline play in the life of a disciple?
2. What is the purpose of discipline?

Psa. 51:16–17; Isa. 1:10–17; 2 Cor. 7:9–11; Luke 18:9–14

3. What is the difference between repentance and penance?
4. How can religious observance dodge the real issue?

Rom. 3:23–5:8; Gal. 1:1–9

5. What part do works and faith play in justification?
6. What is another gospel?

04

A reversal of values
Jonah 1:13–17

'Instead, the men did their best
to row back to land.'
(Jonah 1:13)

o
o
o

We know little about the sailors who manned the ship, but Jonah 1:13 shows them to be thoroughly decent men who wanted to do everything in their power to avoid throwing Jonah overboard. Instead of acceding to his request, they concentrate on rowing as hard as they can towards the shore. The sweat pours from their brows, their arms ache as they pull on the oars, but it is to no avail. The wind continues to blow more fiercely than ever.

To Jonah, the crew were heathens, 'foreigners to the covenants of promise' (see Eph. 2:12), but as they showed their concern for him, he was sharing, whether he felt it or not, a common bond with them – the bond of humanity. I wonder, did Jonah realise as he saw them toiling in their rowing that their concern was not only for themselves but also for him? Jonah was fleeing from God because he did not want to carry the message of God's loving concern to Gentiles. Yet here, before his very eyes, a group of Gentiles were showing more concern and compassion for him than he had for them. They were closer in character to God and to what was right than he was.

Before we begin to feel superior to Jonah with his many failures, perhaps we ought to take a long look at our own attitudes and ask ourselves: Do unbelievers show more compassion and concern for us than we do for them? God wants us to be concerned about all who live in His world regardless of nationality or whether they are saved or lost. R.E. White, the former principal of a Scottish Bible college, once posed this question to his students: 'Why is it so hard for the godly to believe that God also loves the ungodly?' Why indeed.

God also loves the ungodly.

Despite the best efforts of the sailors to reach the shore, the storm proves too much for them and they abandon the task.

Now they have no choice except to do what Jonah suggests. But first they pray to this strange new God. 'Then they cried to the LORD, "O LORD, please do not let us die for taking this man's life" ' (1:14).

It is clear from both their actions and their prayer that they are pinned on the horns of a dilemma. This God is awesome and has tremendous power. He has already caused a fierce storm to blow up because of an act of disobedience by one of His prophets. Obviously He is a God to be reckoned with. Who is to know what He might do to a crew who deliberately throw overboard one of His messengers? These heathen sailors appear to have shown more respect for Jonah's God than Jonah did himself. The prophet was so caught up in self-pity and self-concern that he was unable, in my opinion, to realise that the very thing he was trying to avoid at Nineveh – helping the Gentiles find salvation – is happening before his eyes. The men are slowly but inexorably being won over to the Lord God Almighty.

Jonah's name, by the way, means 'dove'. And a dove, as you know, symbolises peace. The prophet was experiencing very little peace in his own heart at this moment, but God was using his circumstances and his situation to bring peace to the hearts of the heathen sailors. God is able to use our blunders to help others come to know Him. That is a cause for joy and also a cause for sorrow.

God – a Promise-Keeper

Once the sailors have prayed and thrown Jonah overboard, the sea becomes strangely calm – immediately (1:15). The crew can only look at the tranquil sea and each other's faces. It seems too good to be true. Now what will they do? If we suspected that their prayer to Jonah's God was an attempt to get them out of a hole and that they would forget all about Him when their prayer was answered, then we were wrong. Jonah's God has shown He has power over the sea. They are in awe of Him.

All kinds of emotions rise within them: astonishment, gratitude, respect, wonder and relief. What will they do now? We read that 'the men greatly feared the LORD ... offered a sacrifice to the LORD and made vows to him' (1:16). Notice the phrases 'feared the LORD' and 'offered a sacrifice to the LORD'. The repetition of God's covenant name makes it clear that the sacrifices were not to the god of the sea but to the God of Jonah, the One who had so miraculously stilled the storm. Ships often carried live animals to provide both the crew and passengers with fresh meat, so it would have been quite easy to offer this sacrifice.

But in addition to the sacrifice, they made a vow to serve the Lord. How serious were they in making those vows, I wonder? We will never know – this side of eternity at least. Since Jonah was a prophet, no doubt at one time he had made a similar vow to serve God, but he had defaulted on his promise. It is one thing to promise to serve the Lord; it is another to keep that promise. How reassuring it is to know that though sometimes we do not keep our promises to God, He never fails to keep His promises to us.

A whale of a tale

Now we come to the issue which creates problems for many Christians. I refer, of course, to the matter of Jonah being swallowed by 'a great fish' (1:17). C.S. Lewis, for example, could not accept that the story of Jonah was true and considered it to be nothing more than an Old Testament parable. He described it in one place as 'having few historical attachments, grotesque in incidents, and not without a distinct though edifying view of Jewish humour'. I even heard a liberally-minded preacher refer to the story of Jonah as 'a piscatorial conjuring trick'.

Personally, I believe the things we read in the book of Jonah actually happened. We must make clear, though, that the Bible does not tell us (despite the well-known choruses sung in Sunday school) that Jonah was swallowed by a whale. The Hebrew term used is *dag gadol,* which means 'a big fish'. It could have been one of the whale family or it might have been a large fish prepared by God for the purpose. *The NIV Bible Commentary* says: 'Cases are occasionally cited of men recently lost overboard being recovered by whalers, still alive inside their catch.' However, what should clinch the matter is that Jesus Himself referred to the story of Jonah and obviously regarded it as being true. He said, 'For as Jonah was three days and three nights in the belly of a huge fish, so the Son of Man will be three days and three nights in the heart of the earth' (Matt. 12:40).

When we read the story of Jonah we must take into account the fact that God works miracles. First, we see a miracle of timing – God arranges for a great fish to be at the right place at the right time. Second, a miracle of sustenance – Jonah is kept alive for three days.

I fail to understand why people who accept the Old Testament miracles such as the crossing of the Red Sea, the provision of manna in the wilderness and Elijah ascending to heaven in a chariot drawn by horses of fire, balk at the story of Jonah being swallowed by a whale. (By the way, from now on I will refer to the 'great fish' as a whale because it makes for easier reading.) If we look back on the story after having read the New Testament, with its accounts of such miracles as the feeding of the five thousand, the healing of the blind, the stilling of the storm and, of course, the most incredible miracle of all – Christ's resurrection – it becomes difficult to gainsay it.

One writer says that if you believe in a personal God then you have to believe that He can act upon His creation in a way that changes things. 'The sea is his, for he made it, and his hands formed the dry land' (Psa. 95:5). He can suspend the laws of nature or speed them up at will. Every year water is turned into wine in wineries all over the world – a natural process. But one day Jesus speeded up the whole process and did it in minutes. I refer, of course, to the miracle at Cana of Galilee. If God in Christ could do that then, quite frankly, I do not find it difficult to believe that He could cause a man to be swallowed by a whale and sustain him there for three days and three nights. With God, nothing is impossible.

With God, nothing is impossible.

The 'three days' difficulty

We are told that Jonah was inside the whale for a period of three days and three nights (1:17). As we think about this it might be helpful to consider that Jonah found himself inside the great fish for three reasons. First, to save him from drowning. Second, to give him time to come to his senses. Third, to prefigure the death and resurrection of our Lord.

Our Lord, as we have mentioned, referred to the story of Jonah when talking about His death and resurrection (Matt. 12:40).

While reflecting on this time span of three days and three nights it is important to understand the usage of this term in Bible times. The expression did not necessarily refer to three full days. On occasions it was used to denote one full day and part of two others. Some commentators believe that this explains the difficulty a number of people have over the question of how Jesus could be in the tomb three days and three nights when He was put to death on a Friday afternoon (the Sabbath began as the sun went down) and rose again the day following the Sabbath. The explanation offered is that the three days would have included part of Friday afternoon, all of Saturday and part of Sunday morning. A similar sort of reckoning of time in Jewish circles was to think of a week as eight days, which included two Sundays (see John 20:26). Though people like to point out apparent contradictions in the Bible, what they alight upon are not real contradictions, just problems that need thinking through.

Further Study

Ruth 1:1–22; 4:13–17; 1 Cor. 1:18–29; 2 Cor. 4:7; Phil. 1:15–18

1. Who does God choose to serve Him?
2. How does God use unbelievers to help others come to know Him?

John 14:1–3; 14:16–19; 16:33; 2 Cor, 1:20; 7:1; Heb. 6:13–19; 13:5

3. What has God promised you?
4. What have you promised God?

Gen. 4:1–10; Exod. 1:22; Matt. 2:13–18; Acts 5:1–11

5. Think through how we can reconcile the death of Ananias and God's love.
6. Why do the innocent suffer?

05

On talking terms again
Jonah 2:1–4

*'From inside the fish Jonah
prayed to the LORD his God.'*
(Jonah 2:1)

o

o

o

The very first thing the prayerless prophet does when he discovers himself inside the whale is to pray (2:1). But when you think of it, there is very little else he could do there. Do not let this thought, however, detract from the fact that he opened up his heart once again to God. For that we must give him full marks.

We shall see as we examine Jonah's prayer that it is not a prayer for deliverance, but one of thanksgiving. The prophet's heart overflows with gratitude for the spectacular way in which he has been saved from certain death. Some might consider Jonah contemptible for crying out in prayer only when he was in trouble, but such is the mercy and goodness of God that He listens to prayers made in such circumstances nevertheless. Isaac Bashevis Singer, quoted by William Barrett in *The Illusion of Technique*, says, 'Whenever I am in trouble I pray. And since I'm always in trouble, I pray a lot. Even when you see me eat and drink, while I do this, I pray.' It's sad, however, if prayer is limited only to times of trouble. A little boy was asked by his vicar if he prayed every day. 'No,' responded the boy, 'as there are some days when I don't need anything.'

The highest form of prayer is not petition but communion – just talking to God and deepening our relationship with Him. Jonah had not been doing this kind of praying for some time, but now things have changed. He communes with God from inside the fish and is once again on talking terms with the Almighty. He doesn't have much earthly comfort but he has something better – heavenly comfort. There is no comfort like the comfort of a restored relationship with God.

Confined in the whale's stomach, Jonah became a different man. In confinement, I believe, God does some of His greatest work. Have you ever found yourself in a situation you know has been engineered by God in which you can't move one way or the other – where you are hemmed in by Him? 'You have taken me from my closest friends ... I am confined and cannot escape ...' (Psa. 88:8). Why does God put us in such a situation? It is because only then will we stop trying to work things out for ourselves and begin to listen to Him.

All of us are tainted with the terrible tendency to insist on getting our own way. We prefer to act as a god rather than worship the true God. The story that was enacted in the Garden of Eden is re-enacted every day in our homes, offices, factories, shops, boardrooms, schools and colleges. The tempter is at work telling us what he told our first parents in Eden, 'You will be like God' (Gen. 3:5). Confinement is a calculated and deliberate interference with the god-lust that is in us.

When I was a pastor I would hear people say, 'I have been unable to get out for weeks' (perhaps as the result of an accident or an illness). Then they would add, 'It is the best thing that has ever happened to me.' Pressing them for an explanation, I would discover that in the confinement they had woken up to the fact that they had lost touch with God and eternal things. Suddenly, instead of mindlessly pursuing inconsequential matters such as the accumulation of possessions, they came face to face with the reality of who God is. Our lives are not diminished by confinement, but deepened by it. Some of the most profound passages in the New Testament were written by Paul from a prison cell. He was shut up to write immortally.

Prayer that is learned

Now we come to the words of the prayer Jonah uttered from inside the whale. We have already noted that the surprising thing about this prayer is that it is a prayer of thanksgiving and not a prayer of repentance. Does that mean that Jonah had not repented of his disobedience? Was he trying to substitute praise for repentance?

Commentators agree that though there is no mention of repentance in this prayer, Jonah had actually come to the point where he was sorry for his sin. This conclusion is based on the fact that Jonah uses words which are in the past tense: 'In my distress,' he says, 'I called to the LORD, and he answered me' (2:2). Clearly something significant had happened in his soul, though we have no record of it. He continues, 'From the depths of the grave I called for help, and you listened to my cry' (2:2). What we shall find now as we go through Jonah's prayer verse by verse is that it is modelled on the prayers of the psalmists. Almost every verse has words that are borrowed from the vocabulary of the psalms. The book of Psalms, as you know, has two dominant themes: lament and thanksgiving. The writers either cry out in pain or burst forth in praise, and Jonah echoes their thoughts.

He had apparently been nourished by the book of Psalms, and in the midst of a crisis he prayed in the way that others before him had prayed. We, too, would do well to study the intercessions of some of the great prayer warriors of the past. Then, when we can't pray or don't know how to pray, as with Jonah, the prayer language of others will come to our aid.

Jonah's prayer was not so much spontaneous as set, clearly furnished with the stock vocabulary of the psalms. The opening words are taken from Psalm 18: 'I call on the LORD, who is worthy of praise, and I am saved from my enemies' (v.3). They can be found also in Psalm 120:1. One Bible scholar who has studied the phrases used by Jonah in his prayer shows them to be exact quotes from more than a dozen different psalms. And following his study he made this statement: 'Jonah got every word – lock stock and barrel – out of the book of Psalms.'

What does this say to us? It says, I think, that if we want to pray effectively then we need to consider undertaking some apprenticeship in prayer. I thank God for my pastor who told me over and over again in my youth: 'If you want to learn to pray then you need to soak yourself in the book of Psalms. It is the best school of prayer you will ever attend.' And I pass on to you the advice I was given: saturate yourself in the psalms, and when you find yourself in a crisis and don't know how to pray, or what to pray, the words of the psalmists will provide a framework for you. When I am asked what is the best advice I have ever been given, this is what I say: to soak myself in the book of Psalms.

Saturate yourself in the psalms.

There is no doubt that Jonah's prayer was triggered by his plight, but it was not debased by it. He found himself praying a prayer that brought him in touch with the largeness and adequacy of God – a prayer he had learned at the feet of the psalmists.

Another psalm from which Jonah borrows as he gives thanks to God for his protection is Psalm 30. The words 'O LORD, you brought me up from the grave' (Psa. 30:3) are similar to those Jonah uses twice in his prayer: 'From the depths of the grave I called for help' (2:2), and 'You brought my life up from the pit, O LORD my God' (2:6).

A view held by many Christians today is that prayer is true and real only when it is spontaneous. That view needs to be challenged. For twenty centuries the Church in general has used the text of the psalms to teach people and encourage them to pray. Our Christian forefathers explained that fundamentally prayer is our response to the God who speaks to us. His Word must become the basis of everything we do. He must get the first word in – always. Eugene Peterson expresses it like this: 'We come to consciousness in a world addressed by God. We need to learn how to answer, really answer – not merely say Yes sir, No sir ... How do we do this? We don't know the language.

We are so under-developed in this God-addressed world. Israel and the Church put the psalms in our hands and say, "Here, this is the text; practise these prayers so that you will learn the full range ..." '

Every Christian desires to pray. Many echo the words of the Samaritan woman, 'We have nothing to draw with and the well is deep.' Oh but we have – the psalms. Use them as your bucket and you will, I promise you, pull up new strength and inspiration for your prayer life.

The words, '... all your waves and breakers swept over me' (2:3) are from Psalm 42:7. Jonah reflects on the fact that he had been hurled into the deep and was in a desperate situation. But as he muses further he says something quite remarkable: '... all your waves and breakers swept over me'. Notice the words again: '... all *your* waves and breakers swept over me' (my italics).

When we find ourselves in the midst of a storm or buffeted by waves of trouble we are in danger of misunderstanding the meaning of our circumstances. We can view the situation as the refutation rather than the confirmation of God's faithfulness. It behoves us to be careful in seasons of inexplicable trial not to regard the billows as an expression of divine displeasure but as the proof of His concern – concern that we should become the people He wants us to be. When plunged into adversity's icy waters we are apt to forget that it is His waves and His breakers that are sweeping over us. And because of this they cannot harm or hinder, but contribute to the purposes God has for our lives.

We must be careful not to foolishly charge God with neglect or imagine that we have been removed from His keeping when the waves wash over us. Though we might think the billows have been sent to bring us down to death, they are, in fact, meant to bring us into life. The billows God sends will not carry us off course, but sweep us into His arms. A poet put it like this:

Sorrow's seas have swept my soul,
And stripped it of selfish pride,
Yet richer now I stand,
Humbled and purified.

Need a new start?

'I said, "I have been banished from your sight ..." ' (2:4). The words 'banished from your sight' are a further indication that Jonah has actually repented, and is now experiencing once again a close relationship with God. Just as entering a relationship with God isn't possible without repentance, so restoring a broken relationship with Him isn't possible without repentance either. The evidence that Jonah had repented is clearer in this verse than in any other. He tells us that his eye is turned towards the light which he had spurned: 'Yet I will look again towards your holy temple' (2:4).

One of the effects of disobedience is that the soul is filled with a sense of shame. And when we feel shame two things happen. First, we find it difficult to look into the face of the one we have wronged and second, we find it equally difficult to be looked upon by the one we have wronged. Shame has been described by one Christian psychologist as the 'haemorrhaging of the soul'. Our soul bleeds when it is filled with shame and stains every other emotion. Yet there is no sense of shame now in Jonah's soul. For the first time in a long while he admits he is able to look towards God's holy Temple – a statement that implies he is again looking to God for His strength and support. His heart is filled with hope and expectancy; it is a new day and a new beginning.

Is there someone reading these words right now who needs

a new start spiritually? You feel alienated from God because of some sin and your heart is filled with shame. Turn from that sin now, ask God to forgive you, and I promise that through divine forgiveness the shame will be dispelled from your soul and you will look once again into His eyes with joy.

Further Study

Luke 11:1–13; 1 Cor. 2:9–16; Eph. 6:18–19; Phil. 4:4–7; 1 Tim. 2:1–3

1. What are the different types of prayer?
2. What kind do you practise least?

Psa. 42:1–11; Acts 27:9–44; Heb. 6:19

3. How did God meet with Paul in the storm?
4. What is an anchor for the soul?

Psa. 15:1–5; 25:1–22; 51:1–19

5. How do we draw close to God?
6. Meditate on Psalm 145:17–19.

06

A strange prayer chamber
Jonah 2:5–10

*'The engulfing waters threatened
me, the deep surrounded me;
seaweed was wrapped around
my head.*

(Jonah 2:5)

○

○

○

The imagery Jonah uses in the next part of his prayer – 'The engulfing waters threatened me, the deep surrounded me' (2:5) – leads our minds to some of the well-known Bible stories which recount how God's people were menaced by turbulent waters. Think, for instance, of the Flood that covered the earth in the time of Noah, the crossing of the Red Sea and the River Jordan, the squall on the Sea of Galilee, the severe storm which resulted in Paul being shipwrecked on Malta. All these incidents tell us that though the waters were a threat to God's people, they were not allowed to harm them. In each instance God undertook the protection of His people, and did not permit them to be destroyed. This is what Jonah is rejoicing in as he realises that the thunder of the waves and the roar of the sea were powerless to harm him because they were part of God's plan to discipline him and restore their relationship.

When we read the Scriptures we find that God's people offered prayer to Him from some strange places and in some strange circumstances. Paul prayed in a prison. Jesus prayed on a cross. When he was ill, Hezekiah turned his face to the wall and prayed (2 Kings 20:2–3). Daniel no doubt prayed when he was in the lions' den, and Jeremiah is certain to have prayed when he was thrown into an empty cistern. But no one before or after (in Scripture, at least) prayed from the belly of a whale with seaweed wrapped around his head! Not a very comfortable prayer position, to say the least. But prayer, as we said earlier, can be made any time, in any circumstances. Nothing can stop our communication with God. Nothing.

But ...

'Where would we be,' said Dr Martyn Lloyd-Jones on one occasion, 'were it not for the "but's" of the Bible.' He was preaching on Romans 5:8 at the time: 'But God demonstrates his own love for us in this: While we were still sinners, Christ died for us.' So often in Scripture this little conjunction becomes a bridge by which we cross from misery to joy, from spiritual poverty to spiritual plenty.

When Jonah said that he went to 'the roots of the mountains' (2:6) what did he mean? People in Bible days used to think that, like trees, mountains had roots, and that those roots went down into the sea bed. He uses another strange expression also: 'the earth beneath barred me in for ever'. The Living Bible conveys the thought in these words: 'I was locked out of life and imprisoned in the land of death.' Jonah is dwelling here on how close to death he came. But ... *but* ... just as death reached out to grasp him, God in His goodness provided him with a way of escape.

I wonder where you and I would be at this moment *but* for the mercy and goodness of God. It was this knowledge that God would intervene in their lives that saved so many Bible characters from dejection. To them, God was ever present – the great Environing Reality. They never let go of the fact that though God might let them sink down to the very depths of despair, He would, at the last moment, lift them out of it. 'But God.' These two words viewed in their context suggest the thoughtfulness of God and the power of God. It mattered not whether Jonah knew God; God knew him. Jonah was always in His thoughts. So are you, my dear friend. So are you.

It mattered not whether Jonah knew God.

Illuminated memory

'Recollection,' it has been said, 'is often the first step towards realisation.' 'When my life was ebbing away,' confessed Jonah, 'I remembered you, LORD' (2:7). Frequently this God-given sense of memory is what redeems the soul from discouragement and despair. Many a sorely tried person has been brought back to confidence in God by recalling some spiritual experience or memory of the past. Often it is because we forget that we faint. Jonah had been running away from God, and no doubt had attempted to push God out of his thoughts. But as he sinks into the turbulent ocean, the temple of his memory is illuminated by his knowledge of God in the past.

This verse made a particular impact on me shortly before I originally wrote these thoughts on Jonah: 'After he was raised from the dead, his disciples recalled what he had said. Then they believed the Scripture and the words that Jesus had spoken' (John 2:22). Notice that it was when the disciples *recalled* what Jesus had said that they *believed*. Here are two kindred forces that may not be divorced; they form a powerful and fruitful partnership which can be responsible for incalculable good in the life of every believer. Quickened memory often propels the soul to the place of faith in God. This is what happened to Jonah. He remembers the Lord, turns his thoughts once again to Him, reflects on his relationship with Him and the prayer that had previously dried up begins to flow again. This is what an anonymous poet wrote:

How oft in hours of threatened loss,
When heart was numb with many fears,
Has come a flash of light and truth,
Across the interspace of years.

The truth about idolatry
The more Jonah prays, the more profound we see his theology becoming. He thanks God that he does not belong to the ranks of idolaters whose gods are worthless and who

deprive themselves of the blessing that could be theirs: 'Those who cling to worthless idols forfeit the grace that could be theirs' (2:8). One commentator says that this verse is pivotal, for in it Jonah identifies the biggest single hindrance to knowing God – idols.

Jonah was obviously thinking of the idols used by the heathen – idols of wood and stone. But idols can take many other forms too. *Self* can be an idol. *Possessions* can be an idol. *People* can be an idol. Anything that becomes a centre of love and attention – love and attention greater than that which we give to God – is an idol. Idolatry has been described as 'substitution' – substitution of the marginal for the important, the unreal for the Real. Anything or anyone we treat as the object of our absolute loyalty and love takes the place of God. In this sense Jonah, too, was an idolater, for he put his own interests before God, and, as we shall see later, continued to do so, despite the seemingly sincere utterances in his prayer.

One of the devil's tricks is to get us to believe that because we do not bow down, as some pagans do, to idols of wood and stone, we are free from idolatry. Many can offer a prayer similar to Jonah's and thank God they don't worship idols, and then depend on something other than God. When we do this we are just as guilty of idolatry as the heathen. John Calvin saw the human heart as a relentlessly efficient factory for producing idols. Most of us, as we acknowledged earlier, want to be our own god. Any idols in your life I wonder? I found one lurking in mine.

The gift of God

Jonah's mind is made up – apparently: 'But I, with a song of thanksgiving, will sacrifice to you' (2:9). He pledges to go on singing a song of praise to God and promises that when the opportunity arises, he will offer a sacrifice to God and renew his vows. It all sounds so promising but, as we shall see later, Jonah is not as good as his promise. What a mercy it is that God blesses us for what we are today, and does not hold the failures of tomorrow against us.

The climax of Jonah's prayer, when he cries 'Salvation comes from the LORD', is one of Scripture's most wonderful statements. This was one of the great texts used during the Evangelical Revival of the eighteenth century, and is the cornerstone of evangelical **Salvation** truth. I imagine thousands, if not millions, have been converted through hearing this **comes from** text. It was one of Martin Luther's favourite **the Lord.** verses. And it was said that if the great preacher, C.H. Spurgeon, was ever called upon to preach unexpectedly, he would base his sermon on it.

The words have been described as the marrow of the gospel because through them we learn that God is the One who saves us. We can do absolutely nothing to save ourselves. Always the initiative is with God. The very faith by which you take hold of Him is not yours; it is the gift of God. If you have never accepted the salvation which is offered then I plead with you to do so now. This is the good news Jonah sounded out from inside the whale. This is the heart of God's mercy. I sound it again with jubilation: *Salvation comes from the Lord.*

The patience of God

When God decides that the prophet has spent enough time soaking in the whale's digestive juices, He commands it to vomit Jonah up on dry land (2:10). One thing is certain: Jonah emerged from the fish's stomach a better man than when he went in.

But was Jonah a completely changed man as a result of his

time inside the whale? Clearly, the confinement had produced some positive results. It had rid him of the delusion that he could disobey God's commands without suffering the consequences. It had brought him to a place of repentance and restored his relationship with God. But deep down some characteristics remained unaltered: he was still self-concerned and self-justifying. It is a fallacy to think that one event, albeit a significant or traumatic one, can bring about significant changes in our hearts. Sanctification is an ongoing process. There are many things God can do in a moment but, as George Macdonald put it, 'It takes time to make a saint.' Jesus could give sight to the blind – instantly. He could turn water into wine – instantly. He could bring the dead back to life – instantly. But it took time to turn His disciples from weak, vacillating personalities into men who were invincible.

What we should be glad about, however, is that God does not wait until we are perfect before He uses us. If He did, then many of us would have been disqualified years ago. Embedded like splintered glass in Jonah's heart (and also in ours) is a stubborn commitment to independence. God finds some further resistance in His prophet and He sets about removing that. But in the meantime He still has work for him to do. There is nothing more amazing than the patience of God.

Further Study

Gen. 50:20: Rom. 6:15–23; 1 Cor. 2:5–10; Eph. 2:1–10

1. Why does God intervene in our lives?
2. Contrast the person in Ephesians before and after God's intervention.

Psa. 63:1–11; 77:1–20; 78:1–72

3. What is the connection between faith and memory?
4. Why do we forget God's blessings?

2 Cor. 6:16–7:1; Phil. 1:6; 2:12–15; 1 Thess. 4:3–8; 2 Pet. 1:3–11

5. Describe the difference between sanctification and salvation.

6. How does sanctification happen?

07

A second chance
Jonah 3:1–4

'Then the word of the LORD
came to Jonah a second time.'
(Jonah 3:1)

o

o

o

Inside the fish Jonah had made some pretty big promises. Now God is going to take him at his word. The command comes again the second time: 'Go to ... Nineveh and proclaim to it the message I give you' (3:1–2). If Jonah thought that God would change His mind and give him some other task to do he was mistaken. This is the genius of God's Word – it is always the same. What a thrill it is to realise that the grace of God which accepts a repentant heart, seals the act of acceptance with the gift of a new opportunity. The runaway prophet is given a second chance.

How many of us would be where we are today if God had not given us a second chance to participate in His work? Who reading these lines has not been guilty of desertion or defiance of the Lord's commands? Perhaps you are in the situation right now of having wandered off the course set by the divine will and are wondering if God will ever accept you or use you again. You feel disqualified from future service because of past mistakes. Take heart my friend, serving God is not an honour that is earned. None of us qualifies for God's service by merit. It is His mercy, not our merit, that enables us to do anything at all for Him.

If you feel I am describing you at this moment then this message from the Lord is for you: God is giving you another chance. Many of the people we read about in Scripture were given a second chance: David, Elijah, Simon Peter, John Mark, to name just a few. So open your heart now and have done with all self-pity and self-derogation. Tell God you are sorry and be restored to the God-of-the-second-chance.

Grudging obedience

The man who said 'No' now says 'Yes'. God doesn't have to repeat Himself; this time Jonah doesn't argue. He has had enough of disobedience for the time being, so picking himself up and brushing himself down, he sets off for Nineveh in obedience to the word of the Lord (3:3). But what sort of obedience was it? Most commentators feel, as I do, that it was a somewhat reluctant obedience. At this stage, though, we must not be too critical of him; at least he is heading now for Nineveh, not Tarshish.

There is a type of obedience offered by some Christians which is grudging and reluctant. Perhaps that kind of obedience ought not to be called obedience at all. Maybe it's an oxymoron. I came across this statement in my research written by an unknown writer: 'Obedience accepted with delight and authority and exercised with humility provides the very lines along which our spirits best travel.' Obedience enthusiastically and consciously given reverses the scenario which took place in the Garden of Eden. The first human pair disobeyed God and their sin introduced chaos into a perfect world. When we obey God we do the opposite and enable God to work out His purposes – perfectly. C.S. Lewis said that 'Wherever the will is perfectly offered back to the Creator in delight, there is heaven.'

What God longs for is enthusiastic obedience, but as we have seen, He remains patient even when our obedience is shot through with imperfection. Obedience is one of the keys to effective living; feelings come and go. When George Macdonald was asked why we should obey God, he came up with this enigmatic answer: 'To know God is to know that our obedience is due to Him.'

Obedience is one of the keys to effective living.

The great Archbishop William Temple said: 'Every revelation of God is a demand, and the way to knowledge of God is by obedience.' Once Jonah decided to disobey God, he stopped knowing Him; when he decided to obey, then his knowledge of God increased. To know God is to obey Him, and to obey Him is to know Him.

Some time ago a leaflet came into my hands which told this story. A missionary translator was endeavouring to find a word for 'obedience' in the language of the tribe with whom he was working. Apparently there was no word in their language for this virtue; it was something seldom practised. One day while walking through the village the missionary's dog went missing. So putting two fingers in his mouth he gave a loud whistle. Almost immediately the dog appeared and ran to his master's side. A villager looking on said in the local tongue: 'Your dog is all ears.' At once the missionary knew he had found the word for 'obedience'. Are we 'all ears' when it comes to listening to God and obeying His commands?

While preaching once in a church in Dublin, Ireland, I noticed a woman in the congregation with her hand cupped behind one ear. Afterwards she said to me, 'I have been a reader of *Every Day with Jesus* for years, but this is the first time I have ever heard you speak. I didn't want to miss a word.' This is what it means to incline our ears towards God. We cup our hands behind our ears, spiritually speaking, so that not a sound or syllable is missed, and say with eagerness and enthusiasm: 'Speak, LORD, for your servant is listening' (1 Sam. 3:9).

A culture shock

Doubtless as Jonah trekked towards Nineveh his mind was full of questions. How would he be received? What would the citizens say when he told them they were about to be destroyed? And what if they repented and God forgave them? How would he react if people then turned round and accused him of being a false prophet? He did not have long to wait for the answers, for the city lay right in front of him.

Nineveh is first mentioned in the Old Testament as one of the cities established by Nimrod (Gen. 10:9–12), and it became, as we said earlier, the capital of the ancient Assyrian Empire. The book of Jonah describes it as a 'great city', 'a very important city', and also tells us that a visit required three days (3:3). In other words, it would take three days to cover the whole city on foot. Some believe the phrase 'a visit required three days' refers to the administrative district of Nineveh which included the cities of Hatra, Nimrud and Khorsabad as well as the capital. Whichever of these is true, I imagine Jonah experienced a culture shock as he first set foot in Nineveh. One commentator, H.L. Ellison, says, 'To the provincial Galilean familiar with the small, tightly packed Israeli towns on their tells, the wide expanse of Nineveh, including even open land within its walls, must have seemed enormous.'

Jonah had a big task ahead of him. But it had to be done. However, God's enabling is always equal to the task. I saw this once on a poster outside a church: 'The task ahead of you is never as great as the power behind you.' It was a word that spoke directly to me at that time, and I hope it is a word that speaks directly to you now.

The shortest sermon

How, I wonder, did Jonah begin his preaching tour of Nineveh? Did he stop at each street corner as he went along? Did he go to the places where crowds assemble – the markets, for example? Or did he just grab people as they passed him on the street and say, 'God is going to destroy this city in forty days – that is as much time as you have to repent'? We are not told how he went about proclaiming the message, but we are told he began to preach on his very first day there (3:4). Jonah was there to preach and he got on with the task as soon as his feet hit the streets.

Imagine someone walking the streets of any of today's great cities – London, Berlin, New York, Bombay, Lagos, Sydney – and shouting: 'Forty more days and this city will be destroyed.' What do you think would happen?

God's Spirit then took over.

Once when I was in London I saw a man with a placard on which was written: 'This city is doomed. Get out of it as fast as you can.' People smiled as he passed and totally ignored him. They are used to seeing this kind of thing. But the people did not smile when Jonah proclaimed his message. And why? Because it was a message that carried with it the convicting power of God's Holy Spirit. All that Jonah was required to do was to speak the words; God's Spirit then took over and applied the message to the hearts of the people.

Nowadays we would describe these circumstances as a 'revival', or an 'evangelical awakening'. Indeed, what we are about to see in Nineveh is one of the greatest evangelical awakenings recorded in the Old Testament. One of the shortest sermons ever preached – just eight words – brought the biggest response.

Further Study

Judg. 16:13–30; Acts 13:1–5; 15:36–41; 2 Tim. 4:11

1. Differentiate between mercy and merit in serving God.
2. Why does God give us a second chance?

Isa. 20:1–6; Jer. 7:21–29; 11:1–14; Heb. 5:7–10; 10:5–7; 2 Tim. 3:12

3. What did obedience cost Isaiah and Jesus?
4. What will obedience cost you?

Exod. 3:1–4:31; Matt. 28:18–19; 2 Pet. 1:3

5. How were the task and God's power related in Moses' calling?
6. How are they related in you?

08

Facing the future
Jonah 3:5–10

'The Ninevites believed God.'

(Jonah 3:5)

o

o

o

Is there any significance in the fact that Nineveh was given 40 days to repent (3:4)? Why 40? Forty, in Scripture, is a very significant number. 'It is a stock biblical phrase,' says one writer, 'that has hope at its core.' The number 40 is usually used in connection with a period of testing, a time of examination.

The 40 days when the rain fell, creating the Flood which Noah and his family escaped in the ark, was a period of thorough cleansing, a washing away of moral pollution. The 40 years in the wilderness was a probation period for the Israelites, providing them with a training course in discipline and trust. The 40 days when Elijah was on the run from Jezebel following the contest with the priests of Baal swept away the dangerous thoughts that had come into his mind as a result of her threats and intimidation. The 40 days of our Lord's fasting and temptation in the wilderness tested His resolve to do the will of God. Then there also was the 40 days following His resurrection when He demonstrated through numerous appearances to His followers the shape of life in the new kingdom.

In Nineveh the 40-day period of grace had a salutary and sobering effect. It concentrated people's minds on the fact that time was running out. It spelt out doom, but it also spelt out hope. The old Nineveh was to go, but a new Nineveh was possible – a Nineveh whose citizens put their trust in the living God. They didn't have to go on living the way they did. Hope was at hand if they turned their eyes to the living God. Perhaps we need to bring back into modern evangelism the emphasis that time is running out. Maybe that is where we are missing the mark.

Billy Graham said at a conference at which I was present, 'Evangelism devoid of eschatology [the doctrine of judgment and the last things] will get us nowhere fast.' In Nineveh the announcement that the citizens had 40 days to decide whether or not they would turn to God achieved its aim: 'The Ninevites believed God' (3:5). Notice that Jonah did not go about denouncing their sin or taking them to task for their worship of non-existent gods; he focused their eyes on the future. He introduced eschatology into the picture.

The Ninevites were obsessed with the present, taken up with the way things were, but Jonah pointed them to what was to be. Billy Graham is very perceptive – evangelism devoid of eschatology has little bite. The thing that concentrates people's minds is the announcement that the future is bleak without God and that it is better for them to relate to Him now before it is too late. Personally, I believe we are living in the last days and that there is not much time left.

> **The whole world will be judged by Jesus Christ.**

The day is coming when the whole world will be judged by Jesus Christ. This is the message we should be preaching from our pulpits. And the book above all books of the Bible we should be delving into is the book of Revelation.

'The future,' said George Macdonald, 'has its effect on the present.' There is no doubt that an awareness of what lies ahead greatly influences our behaviour in the present. The men and women of this world think the future is in some way magical; they cling to the illusive hope that things will get better. They won't.

A sign for all to see

Was there ever so much contained in such a short sentence: 'The Ninevites believed God'? How effective was the message that Jonah preached. And as a sign that they had truly repented, the people declared a fast and put on sackcloth (3:5).

In ancient times people would go without food or drink for various reasons. If they had done wrong they believed that fasting showed whatever god they worshipped how sorry they were. The Israelites, God's chosen people, would sometimes fast in order to get closer to God, to find out what He wanted them to do, or to demonstrate to Him that they were desperate for His help. The fasting entered into by the people of Nineveh was undertaken to show Jonah's God that they felt remorse for their wickedness and wanted His forgiveness. Often when people fasted they put on sackcloth – a coarse cloth that was meant to symbolise the shame they felt for their sin. Can you imagine a whole city engaged in a fast – the whole population covered in sackcloth? Can you imagine, too, what would happen if a city today were to proclaim a fast and announce that the entire population was turning to God? What a news item that would make.

Somewhere I read that ancient records indicate there was a religious conversion in Nineveh. But we have no need for independent evidence because we have Jesus' words to assure us that the Ninevites' conversion was genuine. This is what He said: 'The men of Nineveh will stand up at the judgment with this generation and condemn it; for they repented at the preaching of Jonah, and now one greater than Jonah is here' (Matt. 12:41).

Not too proud to repent

It isn't only the citizens of Nineveh who turn from their sin to put their trust in Jonah's God; the king is converted too. He rises from his throne, takes off his royal robes, covers himself with sackcloth and sits down in the dust (3:6). He realises that if his city is destroyed then he is destroyed. What is the use of a king without a kingdom? Destruction must be avoided at all costs.

So he issues a royal proclamation. The Living Bible paraphrases his command in this way: 'Let no one, not even the animals, eat anything at all, nor even drink any water. Everyone must wear sackcloth and cry mightily to God, and let everyone turn from his evil ways, from his violence and robbing. Who can tell? Perhaps even yet God will decide to let us live, and will hold back his fierce anger from destroying us' (3:7–9).

The messengers saddle their horses and off they go. They stop only to deliver their message to the citizens of Nineveh. The people are to do without food or drink and the animals too. Desperate situations require desperate measures. Days of inconvenience are as nothing when great issues are at stake. The royal decree set the stage for repentance among the Ninevites. The people were obliged to obey the king's decree outwardly, but there was no way the king could legislate for inward obedience. The people, however, did not need a royal decree to repent; the Spirit of God had already been at work in their hearts and brought them to the point of repentance. They had already believed. A similar revival occurred in my own nation of Wales in 1904. Oh that God would bring revival again – not only in my country but also in yours.

The royal proclamation commanded that all the animals were to be deprived of food also. Why should this be? Surely animals have no consciousness of wickedness and sin.

Withholding food from the animals would have brought grief to their owners and served as an added penance. The inclusion of animals in the fast underlined the depth of repentance that was needed in the city, and thus reinforced the seriousness and solemnity of the moment.

Would to God present-day kings, presidents and political leaders had as much concern for the spiritual well-being of their people, and would likewise encourage them to turn to Him. But if it is too much to expect kings, presidents and political leaders to take a lead in turning to God, it is not too much to expect it of the Church. When we Christians demonstrate to the world our sincere repentance for sin, when we adopt measures that are uncompromising, when we decide that we will take a lead in this matter and put righteousness first, then, though we cannot legislate for righteousness we will, I believe, see a tremendous move of the Spirit of God across many lands. We cannot force salvation on people but we can make it possible for God to act. God will come through a breach. All He asks is for His people to provide Him with an opportunity – then He will make His move.

We can make it possible for God to act.

No hope?

It's deliverance day in Nineveh! The king is delighted, the people are filled with joy. Indeed, everyone in the city is relieved because God has had compassion on them and has forgiven them for their wickedness and sin. 'When God saw ... he had compassion and did not bring upon them the destruction he had threatened' (3:10).

How, I wonder, did they receive the news that God had forgiven them? We are not told. Some commentators believe that God instructed Jonah to tell them the good news, while others believe that He produced in each of the repentant citizens a supernatural awareness that they had been forgiven, in much the same way that those who are truly repentant today sense this.

This might be a good moment to consider the point that Jonah's message was that in 40 days Nineveh would be destroyed, not that in 40 days the city would be destroyed if the people did not repent. A number have speculated that Jonah deliberately made no reference to the need for repentance because deep down in his heart he wanted to see the people of Nineveh destroyed. We cannot be sure of this, of course, and it must be regarded as only a matter of conjecture. However, it does seem strange that there is no record in Jonah's encounter with the Ninevites of a message of hope.

This begs the question: If in fact Jonah did not qualify his message to the people of Nineveh and announce that they could escape impending judgment by way of repentance, then why did the king and his subjects enter into a period of repentance? My guess is that when the Spirit of God is at work in the human heart exposing sin, then that same power, because it is guided by love, also gives the understanding that the way to escape divine wrath is to confess all wrongdoing and throw oneself upon the mercy of a pardoning God.

Further Study

Matt. 24:1–51; Acts 17:30–31; Rom. 13:11–14; 1 Thess. 5:1–10

1. How are doom and hope shown in these passages?
2. How can we reconcile God's mercy and judgment?

Matt. 3:1–8; Eph. 4:17–5:11; James 2:19

3. What indicates true belief?
4. Contrast 'belief' and 'conversion'.

Jer. 24:6–7; Joel 2:12–32; Acts 10:1–48; 16:14

5. What does God promise the sincerely repentant?
6. How does God's Spirit prepare people's hearts?

09

Blocked goals
Jonah 4:1–11

*'But Jonah was greatly
displeased and became angry.'*
(Jonah 4:1)

o
o
o

We come now to the last scenes in the story of Jonah as it is recorded for us in the Bible. Everyone is happy except the prophet. In fact, he is not just unhappy, he is decidedly angry, and enters into an argument with God over the fact that He has seen fit to forgive the Ninevites (4:1). In this final chapter the word 'anger' is mentioned four times in the New International Version and six times in some other translations. It is clearer now than ever that deep down in his heart Jonah wanted the Ninevites destroyed, not forgiven.

Let's examine for a moment how anger arises in the personality. Anger is usually the result of a goal we are pursuing becoming blocked. Let me give you an example. You are all alone in your house and you are woken in the middle of the night with a painful headache. You make your way to the medicine cabinet to get an analgesic and find that the cabinet is locked. You have no idea where the key is and your goal, which is to get a painkiller, is blocked. The likelihood is that to your headache will be added another problem – the problem of anger.

What was Jonah's goal? I think it was this: to see the Ninevites wiped out. He wanted God's goodness to be shown only to Israel. God, in granting forgiveness to the Ninevites, had blocked this goal. Jonah, it seems to me, by nature was not a generous and forgiving person. God had made Jonah in His image, but Jonah had made God in his image – he projected onto God his own mean and parsimonious nature. His God was too small.

His God was too small.

Jonah's real problem
Anger can be an effective diagnostic tool. Just like a red light on the dashboard of a car, it warns us that something is

wrong. Jonah became angry with God because He had blocked his goal of seeing the Ninevites destroyed by offering them His free and full forgiveness. Because things didn't go Jonah's way he became angry and petulant. He prays once more to God, but his prayer is vastly different from the one he prayed inside the whale. Here we see even more clearly his underlying motives and the reality of his true spiritual condition. The Living Bible paraphrases his prayer in a most effective way: 'This is exactly what I thought you'd do, Lord, when I was there in my own country and you first told me to come here. That's why I ran away to Tarshish. For I knew you were a gracious God, merciful, slow to get angry, and full of kindness; I knew how easily you could cancel your plans for destroying these people' (4:2).

Interestingly, he again includes in his prayer excerpts from the Psalms (86:5, 15; 103:8), which first appear in Exodus and Numbers. Jonah appears to have been a good theologian but a bad servant. He was well versed in Scripture but immature in his personality.

One of the things that has interested me down the years in my counselling ministry is that Christians who are good at quoting Scripture are not necessarily good at applying it. They understand the dogmatics of Scripture but don't seem to understand the dynamics of their personality – how they tick. Looking at Jonah from a counsellor's perspective I would say he exemplifies many Christians today: Biblically literate but basically immature.

The great preacher and commentator, John Calvin, in the opening statements of his famous *Institutes* (his defence of his theological beliefs), makes the point that the better we know God the better we will know ourselves, and the better we know ourselves the better we will know God. In my experience most Christians are eager to know God but are not so eager to learn anything about themselves.

Jonah's problem, we said, was immaturity; he had never grown up. His 'inner child of the past' – the part of him that wanted his own way – had not only survived but thrived. He was more concerned about what the people of Nineveh thought of him than how God evaluated him. This childish and immature behaviour was totally inappropriate in a prophet. Clearly, he had never reached the stage which Paul refers to in 1 Corinthians 13: 'When I was a child, I talked like a child, I thought like a child, I reasoned like a child. When I became a man, I put childish ways behind me.' The Greek word Paul uses here for putting away is a powerful one – *katargeo*. It means to render inoperative, to lay aside, to put to rest. Though on the surface Jonah's problem appears to have been a spiritual one, its roots were psychological in the sense that it arose because he was the kind of person who wanted his own way in everything. The temper tantrums he might have displayed in childhood were with him still. We are looking here at a man with a child's attitude; grown up physically but immature spiritually.

Jonah's inner turmoil now leads him to the stage where he wants his life to end. 'Now, O LORD, take away my life, for it is better for me to die than to live' (4:3). If anger is not traced back to the goal that is being blocked and properly dealt with by changing that goal then it can quickly find expression in self-pity, depression and suicidal tendencies. Most psychologists and counsellors know that certain types of depression are the result of anger turned inwards on one's self. This is known in counselling circles as 'retroflexed rage'. People who give vent to their anger rarely get depressed, but when the anger is internalised then it can become a trigger for depression. One psychologist has coined the phrase 'the depressive triad' to explain a certain type of depression. He has found that depressed people, generally speaking, have a jaundiced and negative view of three things: themselves, others and the future.

Jonah, as we see him now, is suffering from 'the depressive triad': he is unhappy with the Ninevites because they had found forgiveness, he is unhappy with himself because his goal has been blocked, and as he looks into the future he sees nothing but trouble working for a God who is eager to forgive. In this condition he pleads with God to take away his life. God's mercy to the Ninevites meant an end (in his view) to Israel's favoured standing. How could he continue in such a situation? Just a little while before, while in the whale's belly, he was rejoicing because he had been delivered from certain death; now he prays to die.

Never forget that one of the greatest barriers to depression is seeing yourself, others and the future from God's point of view. This is one of the best pieces of advice I could ever give you.

Though Jonah wants his life to end, clearly God has other plans. The Almighty has just shown great love and kindness to the people of Nineveh, and now Jonah is about to get a taste of this treatment himself.

How wonderfully God counsels Jonah. Sometimes when I am involved in training counsellors I take them to this passage. God doesn't respond to Jonah by becoming judgmental (a common fault in untrained counsellors) by saying, 'You shouldn't be angry.' Instead He questions him in this way, 'Have you any right to be angry?' (4:4). God brings objectivity to the situation by asking a question rather than making a statement. Jonah, however, does not reply. He is not willing to face up to the roots of his anger and turns away from God as a sulking child would turn away from the concerned questions of his or her parents. Clearly, he is in no mood for a question-and-answer session with God, and becomes one of the most reluctant individuals He ever counselled.

Sulking, Jonah goes off to the east part of Nineveh and waits to see what will happen. But he is not there very long before he finds the sun is a good match for his temper. The heat is unbearable. What is he waiting for as he sits there overlooking the city? Perhaps he is hoping that Nineveh will be destroyed after all. If God had changed His mind once then perhaps He might change it again. I myself am convinced that if fire and brimstone had fallen on Nineveh, Jonah's self-pity would have lifted immediately because his goal would have been reached. How tragic that one of God's prophets should put his own interests before those of his Lord.

Grateful but not changed

In these last few verses Jonah appears such a pathetic figure. Despite having been given the tremendous honour of presenting God's gospel to a Gentile city, he ends up peeved and petulant. The man who has been saved from certain death, has been in and out of a whale's belly, and seen a whole city turn to God, is left feeling sorry for himself. However, something happens that pleases him: he finds some shade.

Sitting under a makeshift shelter he has made, he looks out over the city, and this is where we see God's love once more go into action (4:5). A plant nearby, which most commentators suggest was a castor-oil plant, miraculously grows until its broad leaves provide Jonah with shade and comfort. He has some physical relief at least, if not spiritual solace. I find it interesting as I look through Scripture to see how often God ministers to the physical needs of His servants as He seeks to bring home to them some important spiritual truth. He did that for Elijah, you remember, when He provided food and water for him at the time of his depression (1 Kings 19:1–9). I think also of Simon Peter in the post-resurrection encounter recorded for us in John 21. Having been out all night on the lake, and initially having caught nothing, he was invited by the Lord to enjoy the breakfast He had provided for him. Before confronting him with the important spiritual question, 'Do you love me?', Jesus catered for his physical needs.

Jonah, we read, was 'very happy about the vine' (4:6) – he was grateful but not changed. How sad that even in the presence of a miracle Jonah is still peeved and petulant.

Some physical relief.

Self-pity can sometimes get such a hold on us that not even God can root it out.

Danger!

Jonah's physical and spiritual discomfort is not over. As a new day dawns God arranges for a worm to destroy the plant, and within a short time it withers and dies (4:7). To cap it all, God sends a hot east wind across the plains, and soon Jonah grows faint and once again pleads with Him to take away his life (4:8). One of the saddest things I think I have come across in life is to see a servant of God in such despair that he or she cries out to die, and I have seen this many times. It's strange, isn't it, that a man who has witnessed a whole city turn to God now pleads with that same God to end his existence. His preaching brought success, but he himself was a failure. Can you imagine any evangelist in modern times sitting down after an entire city has been converted and wanting to die? Clearly, God's ministry to him physically and spiritually has not been allowed to touch the core of his life. He is still the same Jonah – self-centred, childish and self-indulgent.

The only explanation for Jonah's continued resistance to the Lord is the fact that there were things on his agenda that were more important to him than the items on God's agenda. He was a runaway and an escapist when we met him in chapter 1, and he is a runaway and an escapist still. He doesn't arbitrarily sever the connection between God and himself, but he separates himself from the Almighty by his petulance and pride.

Whenever we resent God's discipline in our lives, seeking only the prominence that comes through serving Him, we are in great spiritual danger. Surely we need no other warning than that of Jonah.

For a second time God asks Jonah if he has a right to be angry (4:9). This time it is not in connection with Nineveh but with the shrivelled plant. Jonah, however, continues to argue with the Lord. 'Arguing with God,' points out Eugene Peterson, 'is a time-honoured practice.' Many people in the Bible are seen disputing with the Lord. Moses is one who did this. So is Abraham. So is David. So, too, is Job. And Jeremiah, one of the most faithful and loyal of all God's prophets, also reasoned with Him.

One writer I came across, George Campbell, made a statement regarding this matter that at first I was not able to accept. Yet the more I pondered it, the more I realised that it was right. This is what he said: 'Not only is complaint tolerated by God but it can even be the proper stance of a person who takes God seriously.' When we think about it, we may find we frequently argue with God because He doesn't always do things the way we expect. A friend of mine, an Irishman, says (tongue in cheek) that God is Irish because 'everything He says and does seems to be different from everyone else!' But when we come down to it, there is really no point in arguing with God because He is right in everything.

It is amazing to me that God permits us to debate with Him. He has the power to consign us, puny creatures that we are, to utter oblivion, but He has the grace and patience to listen to our arguments, even to debate with us as He did with

Jonah and others. I don't know about you, but I find this quite staggering. A God like this can have my heart any time.

Though Jonah will not face the fact of his anger and seek to find the reason for it, God condescends to explain to him why He caused the plant to wither (4:10). It was an attempt to provide Jonah with a visual aid, something which the Lord could use to reveal to him his wrong attitudes and ideology.

When it is not possible to get a person to see the truth, one has to try to slip past the defences by whatever means possible. Emily Dickinson has a beautiful phrase to describe this type of action: 'Tell the truth but tell it slant.' Jesus, as we know, was expert at telling the truth but telling it slant. Few of His parables mention the name of God, but as people listened to them the truth of what He was saying sunk into their minds nevertheless. The withered plant was God's ploy to get Jonah's attention and to prise him out of the self-pity into which he had fallen. Listen to how the Living Bible paraphrases God's remarks to Jonah: 'Then the Lord said, "You feel sorry for yourself when your shelter is destroyed, though you did no work to put it there, and it is, at best, short-lived. And why shouldn't I feel sorry for a great city like Nineveh ...?" ' (4:10).

Jonah is full of pity for a plant, something that is here today and gone tomorrow, but he has no concern for the spiritual destiny of the people of Nineveh. Does Jonah show any signs of understanding the point God is trying to get across? I'm afraid not. God has gone as far as He can go. He will seek to persuade but He will never coerce. He will respect the right of a person to say 'No' to the last.

God so loved ...
The story of Jonah has no proper ending. It closes with an unanswered question. The chapter began with Jonah arguing

with God under the short-lived plant and ends with God asking him this haunting question: 'Should I not be concerned about that great city?' (4:11). Did Jonah ever answer this question, I wonder? If so, what did he say?

We will never know, for his answer, if indeed there was one, is not recorded. I would love to find out, and I am sure you would too, if Jonah ended his quarrel with God, if he ministered to God's people in Nineveh, or if he returned to Joppa and boarded another ship bound for Tarshish. Why does the author not tell us? Some feel a part of the original manuscript is missing, hence the abrupt ending. I do not believe that is the case. I think, rather, it is the intention of the author to leave the question hanging in the air. It is part of the storyteller's art. The reason there is no answer is to leave us room to provide our own answer – a personal answer.

So now we must stop being curious about how Jonah answered God's question and give our own response to it.

A glimpse into the immense world of God's grace. How do we feel about a God who loves those whose lives are full of sin and wickedness? Are we more interested in seeing them get their just deserts than in finding pardon and forgiveness? Hopefully, through the story of Jonah, we have had a glimpse into the immense world of God's grace. The story focuses our gaze afresh on the fact that the God we serve and worship loves not just one particular race or group of people, but the whole wide world.

> *O Father, with all my heart I answer, 'Yes, dear Lord, it is right that You should be concerned.' Draw me closer than ever to Your heart so that Your concern for the lost might become my concern too. In Jesus' Name I ask it. Amen.*

Further Study

Num. 11:1–15; 1 Kings 19:1–14; Job 7:1–16; Psa. 43:1–5

1. How do we see 'the depressive triad' in Moses, Elijah and Job?

2. Is there an antidote?

Isa. 1:18; Gen. 18:16–33; Jer. 12:1–17; 15:15–21

3. How do we benefit by debating with God?

4. How does He benefit?

Luke 19:1–10; John 3:16; 2 Cor. 4:1–7; 5:14–21

5. How concerned is God about the lost?

6. How concerned are you?

National Distributors

UK: (and countries not listed below)
CWR, Waverley Abbey House, Waverley Lane, Farnham, Surrey GU9 8EP.
Tel: (01252) 784710 Outside UK (44) 1252 784710

AUSTRALIA: CMC Australasia, PO Box 519, Belmont, Victoria 3216.
Tel: (03) 5241 3288

CANADA: Cook Communications Ministries, PO Box 98, 55 Woodslee
Avenue, Paris, Ontario Tel: 1800 263 2664

GHANA: Challenge Enterprises of Ghana, PO Box 5723, Accra.
Tel: (021) 222437/223249 Fax: (021) 226227

HONG KONG: Cross Communications Ltd, 1/F, 562A Nathan Road, Kowloon.
Tel: 2780 1188 Fax: 2770 6229

INDIA: Crystal Communications, 10-3-18/4/1, East Marredpally,
Secunderabad – 500 026. Tel/Fax: (040) 7732801

KENYA: Keswick Books and Gifts Ltd, PO Box 10242, Nairobi.
Tel: (02) 331692/226047 Fax: (02) 728557

MALAYSIA: Salvation Book Centre (M) Sdn Bhd, 23 Jalan SS 2/64,
47300 Petaling Jaya, Selangor.
Tel: (03) 78766411/78766797 Fax: (03) 78757066/78756360

NEW ZEALAND: CMC Australasia, PO Box 36015, Lower Hutt.
Tel: 0800 449 408 Fax: 0800 449 049

NIGERIA: FBFM, Helen Baugh House, 96 St Finbarr's College Road, Akoka,
Lagos. Tel: (01) 7747429/4700218/825775/827264

PHILIPPINES: OMF Literature Inc, 776 Boni Avenue, Mandaluyong City.
Tel: (02) 531 2183 Fax: (02) 531 1960

REPUBLIC OF IRELAND: Scripture Union, 40 Talbot Street, Dublin 1.
Tel: (01) 8363764

SINGAPORE: Armour Publishing Pte Ltd, Block 203A Henderson Road,
11–06 Henderson Industrial Park, Singapore 159546.
Tel: 276 9976 Fax: 276 7564

SOUTH AFRICA: Struik Christian Books, 80 MacKenzie Street, PO Box 1144,
Cape Town 8000. Tel: (021) 462 4360 Fax: (021) 461 3612

SRI LANKA: Christombu Books, 27 Hospital Street, Colombo 1.
Tel: (01) 433142/328909

TANZANIA: CLC Christian Book Centre, PO Box 1384, Mkwepu Street, Dar es
Salaam. Tel/Fax (022) 2119439

USA: Cook Communications Ministries, PO Box 98, 55 Woodslee Avenue,
Paris, Ontario, Canada Tel: 1800 263 2664

ZIMBABWE: Word of Life Books, Shop 4, Memorial Building,
35 S Machel Avenue, Harare. Tel: (04) 781305 Fax: (04) 774739

For email addresses, visit the CWR website: www.cwr.org.uk

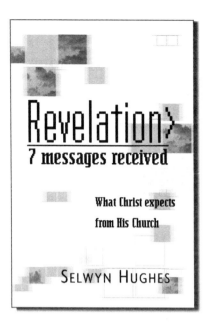

What is God saying to the Church?

 If you want to know what God is saying to the Church in this century then you need to know what He said to the Church in the first century.

Revelation: 7 Messages Received explores each letter to the churches of Asia in depth; it is a contemporary look at a classic text for people of today. This could mark a significant spiritual development both in you and in the church where God has placed you.

* Ideal for personal or group study
* Further Study section with each chapter
* Bible references and discussion starters

£3.99 ISBN: 1-85345-204-1

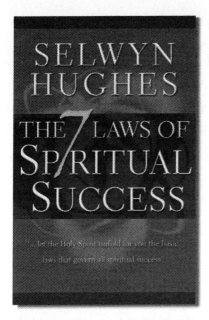

The one book that could forever change your life

Just as there are laws in nature that hold our physical world together, so there are laws for life that make our spiritual walk a success.

In *The 7 Laws of Spiritual Success* Selwyn Hughes draws on a lifetime's experience in counselling and pastoral work to deliver seven essential principles that are relevant and effective for every man and woman, and for every generation.

* The primary place of worship
* The need to live in thankfulness
* The importance of forgiveness
* The value in perseverance
* The role of servanthood
* The doorway of repentance
* The cultivation of our spiritual life

£7.99 ISBN: 1-85345-237-8

Trusted
All Over the World

Daily Devotionals

Books and Videos

Day and Residential Courses

Counselling Training

Biblical Study Courses

Regional Seminars

Ministry to Women

CWR have been providing training and resources for Christians since the 1960s. From our headquarters at Waverley Abbey House we have been serving God's people with a vision to help apply God's Word to everyday life and relationships. The daily devotional *Every Day with Jesus* is read by over three-quarters of a million people in more than 150 countries, and our unique courses in biblical studies and pastoral care are respected all over the world.

For a free brochure about our seminars and courses or a catalogue of CWR resources please contact us at the following address:

CWR,
Waverley Abbey House,
Waverley Lane,
Farnham,
Surrey GU9 8EP

Telephone: 01252 784700
Email: mail@cwr.org.uk
Website: www.cwr.org.uk